T0063332

26.2

—A MARATHON OF
CHRISTIAN
DEVOTIONS

Learning Life's Lessons Through Running

CHRIS MEIKEL

WESTBOW®
PRESS
A DIVISION OF THOMAS NELSON
& ZONDERVAN

WestBow Press books may be ordered through
booksellers or by contacting:

WestBow Press
A Division of Thomas Nelson & Zondervan
1663 Liberty Drive
Bloomington, IN 47403
www.westbowpress.com
1 (866) 928-1240

Because of the dynamic nature of the Internet, any web addresses or
links contained in this book may have changed since publication and
may no longer be valid. The views expressed in this work are solely those
of the author and do not necessarily reflect the views of the publisher,
and the publisher hereby disclaims any responsibility for them.

Any people depicted in stock imagery provided by Thinkstock are
models, and such images are being used for illustrative purposes only.
Certain stock imagery © Thinkstock.

Scripture taken from the New King James Version. Copyright 1979, 1980,
1982 by Thomas Nelson, inc. Used by permission. All rights reserved.

ISBN: 978-1-4908-5799-2 (sc)
ISBN: 978-1-4908-5800-5 (e)

Library of Congress Control Number: 2014919135

Printed in the United States of America.

WestBow Press rev. date: 11/21/2014

Foreword

We've all had days where we have felt too tired to run. Too weary. The day has been too full. Yet, we know that if we actually go out the door we'll feel more refreshed. We will feel more revived. Sometimes, it can be the same set of excuses in our spiritual walk. Our prayer life or our devotion times suffer because we "don't have time" or are "just too tired." Yet we know, again, that if we spend that time with God we are refreshed in His very presence.

There are many times in life where we find ourselves challenged to go beyond ourselves. It's interesting how God puts other people in our lives to help us accomplish these tasks. Many times, it's the encouragement of others that allow us the blessing of accomplishing what we may have never done on our own. Perhaps it's running four laps around that new blacktop high school track. Running a 5K for a PR. Maybe it's running a marathon. Perhaps your goal is to go deeper into a rich walk with our Lord and Savior Jesus Christ. Oftentimes, it's the encouragement of others that helps you achieve and surpass your goals.

It takes discipline to consistently be in God's Word. It takes discipline to be a runner as well. You can't simply attend a church service once a week and expect great spiritual depth as a result. We need daily communication with Jesus to go deeper in our relationship with Him. We need more than a once a week spiritual "workout." If you want to know God and His will, you consistently have to spend time with Him. Similarly, you can't just run one day a week and expect results. Oh, sure, you can run one day a week and call yourself a runner. I have no problem with that. In fact, I applaud you for joining the club. But, if you want to go further, go faster, or accomplish a weight loss or a time goal there simply has to be some consistency.

Blending his passions for running and for time spent in devotion with God, Chris talks freely about some real life personal running experiences. Scripturally grounded, his devotion keeps you focused on God's Word as your source of strength and endurance. Let's face it: runners need endurance and runners need prayer. In any given marathon there are a lot of people praying. Some runners pray the simple prayer, "Lord, get me through this!" Marathoners pray the night before, "Lord, let me sleep tonight." And after, "Lord, heal this aching body!"

Chris offers the consistency of his life experiences alongside the truth of God's Word. Chris has a consistent walk. He's consistent in his radio ministry. He's consistent in his running. Consistent with his gift of encouragement to others. In this book he shares thoughts that will help you make it through the day, through the dreaded long a beautiful, stable structure ready to meet the day-to-day living demands of our family.

The blueprint for success in running and in your life in Christ is very similar to that. As a runner, you've built a foundation through years and years of training. Mile after mile, the groundwork was laid as you prepared for your first test, a five kilometer run. Over time, you've continued to build on that foundation, then cosmetically added speed work, a change of diet, and maybe weight training, hoping to get faster, or possibly test yourself at a greater distance. After all the planning, preparation and construction, the result is a fit athlete, ready to meet the demands of whatever challenges you put your body through.

In Matthew 7:24-27, Jesus reminds us to build upon a strong foundation in our walk with Him. It says, "Therefore whoever hears these sayings of Mine, and does them, I will liken him to a wise man who built his house on the rock: and the rain descended, the floods came, and the winds blew and beat on that house; and it did not fall, for it was founded on the rock. But everyone who hears these sayings of Mine, and does not do them, will be like a foolish man who built his house on the sand: and the rain descended, the floods came, and the winds blew and beat on that house; and it fell. And great was its fall."

In whatever you do, start with a firm foundation and realize that the formula for success will always include ample preparation. The words of former president Abraham Lincoln emphasize exactly that. He said, "Give

Introduction

THE FIRST TWO HOUSES I OWNED IN ST. JOSEPH, MISSOURI WERE PRE-existing structures, modest homes that met the needs of our growing family. Eventually, we made the decision to build a new home on the outskirts of town. After a number of meetings with the builder, we selected our lot, chose the style and floor plan, and signed the papers.

From there, the construction process began. As you might imagine, it didn't start with hammers and nails, two by fours, and the sound of whining saws. Cosmetic features like oak cabinets, light fixtures, and ceramic tile were weeks and weeks away. Instead, powerful bulldozers and backhoes moved thousands of pounds of earth. Their job was to prepare the ground so forms could be set to pour the concrete for the house's foundation.

We drove by almost on a daily basis to see what progress had been made as walls went up, the roof was erected, and the house enclosed. The process continued with plumbing and wiring, drywall and trim, and primer and paint. Carpet went down on the floors and fresh sod was laid in the yard. After weeks and weeks of planning, preparation, and construction, the result was

runs, and through the obstacles that running and life put in your path.

What I know about Chris is that he is passionate. He's passionate about his relationship with Jesus, his Lord. Passionate about going deeper and taking others with him. He's passionate about running. He's done a masterful job blending his loves. This devotion will help you with your walk with Jesus. It will help you with your running. The only thing stopping you from becoming a more consistent runner and from becoming a more consistent servant of Christ is time. My prayer is that you will take the time to listen to God's voice as you go through this devotion and go through any of your upcoming runs. My prayer is that you would be encouraged, uplifted, and challenged not just as a runner, but as a Christian.

In your Christian walk and in your running may you "run and not grow weary." Isaiah 40:31

Pastor Dennis Jennings

me six hours to chop down a tree and I will use the first four sharpening the axe." Author Alan Armstrong penned this, "Champions do not become champions when they win the event, but in the hours, weeks, months and years they spend preparing for it. The victorious performance itself is merely the demonstration of their championship character." And Pastor Robert Schuller reminds us that preparation will not be glamorous. He said, "Spectacular achievement is always preceded by unspectacular preparation."

But our challenges as Christians go far beyond a 10k or marathon. Paul's emphasis on preparation comes from Ephesians 6:13-18. "Therefore take up the whole armor of God, that you may be able to withstand in the evil day, and having done all, to stand. Stand therefore, having girded your waist with truth, having put on the breastplate of righteousness, and having shod your feet with the preparation of the gospel of peace; above all, taking the shield of faith with which you will be able to quench all the fiery darts of the wicked one. And take the helmet of salvation, and the sword of the Spirit, which is the Word of God; praying always with all prayer and supplication in the Spirit, being watchful to this end with all perseverance and supplication for all the saints."

Your readiness will always begin with a strong foundation that you continue to build upon with consistent preparation. As a runner and as a Christian, you will find success if you keep these three simple words in the proper order.

Prepare. Endure. Finish.

1

Transformation

IT WAS A QUIET SATURDAY EVENING AT HOME FOR BEN AND THERESA. A family photo album was their entertainment, bringing far more enjoyment than anything the television had to offer. Their nearly 25 year relationship yielded photographs beginning with their high school prom, then college graduation, wedding photos, children's birthdays, Christmas, and family vacations. A couple of photos caught Ben's attention. One, standing shirtless and muscular just out of high school, Ben jokingly flexed, displaying his shapely chest and chiseled arms. A second photo, taken at their ten year class reunion, revealed that Ben's shapely chest had sunk to his waistline, his face was full, and missing was that healthy, glowing youthfulness that 35 additional pounds had seemingly stolen away.

That same night at the reunion Ben's eyes were opened; a few weeks later, so was his heart. He'd lost touch with Gary Stevens, whose physique prompted the "you look great" comment from more than one fellow alum. It also provoked the "how'd you do it" question from Ben. Gary was more than willing to share his running testimony, at the beginning nothing more than a glorified jogger, then building on that foundation mile after mile. Ten years removed from Langston High, Gary's running resume included two marathons, four halves, and countless 5Ks and 10Ks.

Their Friday night conversation led to a Saturday morning run. It was the first of many daily workouts for Ben, and the two continued to meet regularly on the weekends. Ben also noticed another change in Gary. Gone was the brashness of his youth, and the vulgar language that used to accentuate his conversation. Gary talked about his faith in Jesus Christ, and while running had become an important part of his life, it was his relationship with God that had the greatest impact. Gary shared a scripture from 1 Timothy 4:8 which says, "For bodily exercise profits a little, but godliness is profitable for all things, having promise of the life that now is and of that which is to come." He knew that the physical transformation had short term value, but that godliness is profitable now and for eternity.

Five years later at the 15-year reunion Ben was the one on the receiving end of the "you look great" comments and fielding the "how'd you do it" questions. While his physical transformation brought about a new confidence, he knew that spiritually he wasn't complete without Christ in his life. And it was on that quiet Saturday evening at home that he and Theresa cherished most a photo of Ben, his shirt wet and clinging to his fit body, as he resurfaced after being submerged in the church baptismal. The transformation was now complete.

Additional Suggested Scripture

2 Corinthians 5:17

2

Pure and Simple

RUNNER AND AUTHOR MARK WILL-WEBER ONCE WROTE, "RUNNING IS real and relatively simple...but it ain't easy." While that statement might make your high school English teacher cringe, its essence is right on the money.

Here's another statement, this time grammatically correct, that you might also agree with..."Running is the purest form of athletic competition."

Think about it. You don't need any ball or goal. It doesn't require gloves, racquets, bats, clubs, nets, helmets or any other special equipment. You can roll out of bed in the morning, slip on your running shoes - which Zola Budd proved in the 1984 Summer Olympics are also optional - and head out the door.

You don't need an opponent. No special playing field is necessary with a three point line or double's alley. No timeouts or overtimes, no annoying whistles or buzzers. Just a starting point and a finish line. That's all you need. Nothing else needs to be added.

I think you will quickly agree with the statement, "Running is the purest form of athletic competition."

Spiritually, you can't become complete without the purity of God's Word. In 2 Timothy 3:16-17 it says, "All scripture is given by inspiration of God, and is profitable for doctrine, for reproof, for correction, for instruction in righteousness, that the man of God may be complete, thoroughly equipped for every good work."

And keep this in mind every time you open your Bible, what we read in Proverbs 30:5-6, "Every word of God is pure; He is a shield to those who put their trust in Him. Do not add to His words, lest he rebuke you, and you be found a liar."

God's Word is simple and pure, even in the midst of life's complexities.

Additional Suggested Scripture
1 John 3:2-3

3

All the Right Things

MEET LARRY. I'VE SEEN HIM AT A NUMBER OF RACES IN THE AREA. HE stands about 5-10, slight build, virtually no muscle definition. He seems to be at every 5K I run, so I'm guessing Larry "races" quite frequently.

Larry lives the runner's life. His pre-race ritual is to talk to anyone who will listen about, what else, running. He talks of his 70 mile weeks, or how he's incorporated more speed work into his training. His analysis of races he's run in the past month or so are painfully thorough, apparently an attempt to lull any competitors in his age group into a pre-race coma.

Larry, of course, dresses the part. He's *New Balance* from head to toe: shoes, socks, shorts, matching singlet and mesh hat. And the ensemble wouldn't be complete without the watch and heart rate monitor strapped on his wrist.

Larry hears the starter's instructions and assumes his starting stance. The hundreds of others around him mid-pack stand straight up, knowing that they won't move for ten to 15 seconds once the gun fires. As Larry and the others reach the starting line, he clicks his watch, knowing how important split times are when you're running a 26 minute 5K.

Seven minutes after filing my way through the finishing chute, I turn to see Larry struggling toward the finish line, his head bobbing and arms flailing. The extra training miles and added speed work seem to have added little, if anything, to his finishing kick. He lunges toward the line, with his chest extended, and clocks another 26 minute finish.

There was a time when my Christian walk bore a strong resemblance to that description of Larry. Outwardly, it appeared I was doing all the right things: reading my Bible, looking the part, placing myself among the crowd that was "running" with God. But when I was out there on my own, I was struggling, displaying the Christian equivalent of the bobbing head and flailing arms.

In Galatians 5:22-25 it says, "But the fruit of the Spirit is love, joy, peace, longsuffering, kindness, goodness, faithfulness, gentleness, self control. Against such there is no law. And those who are Christ's have crucified the flesh with its passions and desires. If we live in the Spirit, let us also walk in the Spirit." Are you seeing those kind of results in your walk with Christ? Join your life to His and see the fruit of the Spirit grow in you.

Additional Suggested Scripture
Micah 6:8

4

Little Rock

The streets of Little Rock, Arkansas looked rather inviting on that Sunday morning. More than a thousand runners accepted the invitation for the capital city's inaugural marathon in 2003. It was more than just the demand of 26 miles and change that would test each runner's endurance. Running great Bill Rodgers was there and the course left an impression on him. He said, "Any marathon worth its salt has a few hills. Little Rock is a little salty."

Your first marathon should come with a warning label; *Be prepared for anything. More than just your endurance will be tested.* Your months, or even years of training for this moment only partially prepare you for the grueling test that lies ahead. You heard the stories from seasoned marathoners about how rewarding it is, crossing the finish line after hundreds or thousands of others, yet still feeling victorious in your accomplishment.

What they didn't tell you was that completing the course would require overcoming leg cramps beginning at mile 17. They forgot to mention that a blister would develop on your left heel, and that your dry, lightweight singlet would become soaked with sweat and feel like a weighted vest. Nobody mentioned the battle waged between mind and body that makes you have to think about every step you take.

At mile 19, a well-intentioned woman shouted, "You can do it!" Her confidence in me far-exceeded my own. Then at the 20 mile mark, a middle aged guy with a sandwich in one hand and a can of Coke in the other shouted, "Hang in there, only six more miles to go." There's a comforting thought.

Down the road as I drew closer to the finish line, I realized their intentions were good. Too often, as Christians, we look for ways to minister to others, yet we make ourselves unreceptive to the blessings that others want to bestow upon us, even if it's only a brief word of encouragement from a complete stranger.

In Hebrews 10:24-25 it says, "And let us consider one another in order to stir up love and good works, not forsaking the assembling of ourselves together, as is the manner of some, but exhorting one another, and so much the more as you see the Day approaching."

Additional Suggested Scripture
John 12:1-8

5

Great Design

It's been almost two years since Dave began documenting his daily runs. His running journal was filled with his day-to-day activities on the roads, on the track, and on the trails around his home. It was mostly statistical data, weather conditions and geographical information that he recorded. Tuesday's entry said, "Ran a half mile warm up, then seven miles at about a 7:30 pace, then a half mile cool down. Temp was in the mid 70s with just a little breeze. Felt good throughout, and especially strong at the end."

But Wednesday was different. Missing were mileage totals and the daily weather report. Instead he wrote, "I stopped in the middle of my workout and began walking with my arms extended towards heaven praising God. I was overcome by the revelation that God has anatomically designed my body to do incredible things. It has hundreds of bones and muscles, tendons and ligaments, a heart and lungs, and more miles of blood

11

vessels than most humans will run in a lifetime. And for nearly an hour, the most incredible machine every designed, the human body, performed flawlessly. I praise You because I am fearfully and wonderfully made."

The numbers are staggering: 206 bones in the adult body, approximately 640 muscles, thousands of miles of intestines and veins, not to mention a brain, heart and lungs, a stomach, kidney and liver. And without even a thought how it all works together, every day Dave stepped out of his home's front door and put it to the test. Only today, he stopped to praise its Designer and Creator, in awe of its complexity, and thankful that it can endure the daily workouts he puts it through.

That day Dave made no effort to stop the sweat from his body from dripping onto the journal's pages. The body's cooling system, he realized, was just another incredible feature of our Creator's great design.

Have you stopped to thank Him today?

Additional Suggested Scripture
1 Thessalonians 5:16-18

6

No Regrets

RELUCTANTLY. THAT'S HOW I BEGAN RUNNING. IT WAS THE SUMMER OF 1972. I stood in our high school's weight room, the smell of sweat having permeated every square inch of the facility. The sound of clinking weights and grunting football players echoed throughout the room, each attempting to showcase his manliness with every vein-popping repetition. After ten minutes, never having lifted a weight, I retreated without regret, knowing that my five foot seven, 98-pound frame needed to find another activity.

My older brother and varsity football player, suggested cross country. Really, me, a runner. It wasn't like I could avoid the coach. His name was prominently displayed on my class schedule as my science teacher.

Practice started, and while that football weight room was intimidating, it hardly compared to the prospect of me running four or five miles. The leg cramps I experienced the first week were so intense, that I questioned whether I received a full dose of my polio vaccination. As we've all found out as runners, it's amazing what training and conditioning will do. That reluctance soon dissipated and now, thousands of miles later, there's not even one ounce of regret.

For many of us, our Christian walk came much the same way, reluctantly. Thank God for new beginnings. Ephesians 5:8 says, "For you were once darkness, but now you are light in the Lord." And Paul encourages "Christian conditioning" in Colossians 2:6-7 where he writes, "As you therefore have received Christ Jesus the Lord, so walk in Him, rooted and built up in Him and established in the faith, as you have been taught, abounding in it with thanksgiving."

Perhaps reluctant to begin, but thousands of miles into my Christian walk, there's not one regret.

Additional Suggested Scripture
Acts 9:1-20

7

24 Hours

LIKE MOST SATURDAYS, THIS ONE BEGAN WITH AN EARLY MORNING RUN. The sun began to shine brightly as it peeked above the eastern horizon. The forecast called for a predominately clear sky, with the heat of the day about five hours away following a relatively cool May morning. Three teams of ten knew little about what lied ahead. The distance they'd run was uncertain. Amazingly, they could see the entire course from where they stood, and the finish line would never be more than 200 yards away from where they started.

The site was a track at a junior high school in Kansas City, Kansas. At 8 a.m. sharp one runner from each team began what would be thousands of laps around the asphalt oval. Each runner would run a mile before handing off to another teammate, and for 24 hours that process would continue. When it came your turn, you ran your mile. You guessed it...a 24 hour relay.

Hour after hour, mile after mile, we wore a groove in the track's inside lane. And like many endurance events, this one proved to be too much for too many. Our team of ten would shrink to nine at 6 p.m. Then to eight the next hour. Two hours later we were down to seven. And shortly thereafter, a half dozen high schoolers were left to fill the void for those final ten hours. Your turn on the track came more often, which meant more miles and less rest.

Into the wee hours of the morning we ran toward the lanterns positioned in each dark corner of the track. Four a.m., 5 a.m., 6 a.m., and finally 7 a.m. Just an hour to go. Our legs weary, our bodies fatigued, our minds thoughtless, we pressed on. Finally, 24 hours since we began, each of us having logged more than a marathon distance of miles, we finished what we started.

In Philippians 1:6 Paul writes, "being confident of this very thing, that He who has begun a good work in you will complete it until the day of Jesus Christ."

Additional Suggested Scripture
Romans 5:1-6

8

The Race Set Before Us

AMERICAN TOMMIE SMITH STOOD ATOP THE VICTORY PODIUM AT THE 1968 Summer Olympics in Mexico City, having just won the gold medal in the men's 200 meters in world record time. But it was the drama that he and bronze medalist and fellow American John Carlos created shortly thereafter that most people remember. The two bowed their heads and each hoisted a black-gloved fist in the air as the American anthem played, a silent protest again racial discrimination.

Four days later, John Stephan Akhwari also created high drama. The Tanzanian distance runner was representing his country in the Olympic marathon. Not having trained in high altitude, he struggled with the conditions and began to experience leg cramps early in the race. Then, near the 12 mile mark, Akhwari fell badly while jockeying for position among a group of runners, wounding his knee and injuring his shoulder. But he was determined to finish.

The Olympic stadium, filled with 80,000 spectators when the marathon began, now housed only the few thousand that remained. With his leg heavily bandaged, and limping quite noticeably, Akhwari completed the course, finishing last among the 57 that completed the race, more than an hour after the winner broke the tape.

The small crowd that remained respectfully cheered as the wounded warrior crossed the finish line. Later, when he was interviewed, Akhwari was asked why he continued running despite his predicament. Akhwari said, "My country did not send me 5000 miles to start the race; they sent me 5000 miles to finish the race."

In Hebrews 12:1-2 it says, "Therefore we also, since we are surrounded by so great a cloud of witnesses, let us lay aside every weight, and the sin which so easily ensnares us, and let us run with endurance the race that is set before us, looking unto Jesus, the author and finisher of our faith, who for the joy that was set before Him endured the cross, despising the shame, and has sat down at the right hand of the throne of God."

Additional Suggested Scripture
Isaiah 40:29-31

9

Competitive

IF THERE'S A MORE COMPETITIVE SOCIETY IN THE WORLD THAN IN America, I'd like to see it. Or maybe I wouldn't. We love to compete, and we definitely love to win.

How many times have you seen two guys entered in a road race who train together day after day. They arrive in the same vehicle, stretch and warm up together, run at a conversational pace the entire race, stride for stride, and then turn a 5K into a 100 meter dash, both of them determined to beat the other to the finish line? We're competitive!

I love to compete. It's part of the beauty of the American road racing scene. No matter what your age is, you can compete against your peers. Granted, not all runners are like that. Some are content with the physical benefits that come from running. Others have training partners and enjoy the socializing and camaraderie. Me, I love to compete. I don't think I'll ever be content with just going through the motions in a 5K or 10K. I train way too hard for that.

Too bad as Christians we don't compete for souls like we do for medals and trophies.

Jesus says in Matthew 9:37-38, "The harvest truly is plentiful, but the laborers are few. Therefore pray the Lord of the harvest to send out laborers into His harvest."

In 2 Peter 3:9 the apostle reminds us that "The Lord is not slack concerning His promise, as some count slackness, but is longsuffering toward us, not willing that any should perish but that all should come to repentance." We need to get in the game and start competing for souls.

And finally, we find this in the book of Proverbs, in Chapter 11 and verse 30. It reads, "The fruit of the righteous is a tree of life, and he who wins souls is wise."

Additional Suggested Scripture
Mark 16:14-16

10

Conversational Pace

TAKE JUST A MOMENT TO CONSIDER WHAT YOUR FAVORITE WORKOUT IS. For some, it would take you along a certain route, possibly tree-lined, relatively flat, and pleasing to the eye from start to finish. Some would picture a trail run, challenging every step of the way, even treacherous in some areas. Or maybe you've got a speed workout that, although it places great demand on your body, the benefits derive tremendous satisfaction.

Sometimes though, it's best to just call a friend, schedule something rather informal; a leisurely jaunt where you can catch up on what's happening in each other's lives at a "conversational pace."

That's what I think God wants us to do in our relationship with Him. Live it at a "conversational pace."

So many times in Scripture we find the Christian life compared to a walk, not running or at a standstill. Relationships that are hurried rarely have much substance. Yet many of us treat our relationship with

God in just that way. Our Bible reading and prayer time become an obligation that we squeeze in at the end of our day, like Johnny Carson used to do with his last guest on the *Tonight Show.*

Allow God to speak to you through His Word. Pray and listen. Discover the things that you're missing because of the life pace that you've established for yourself. More than once I've noticed things while on foot during a daily run that I missed while passing by in my car at 40 or 50 miles per hour. Maybe you can relate to that. We live our lives in much the same way. Slow down. Live life at a "conversational pace."

Additional Suggested Scripture
Matthew 6:5-13

11

Think Before You Speak

ONCE I DEPART MY NEIGHBORHOOD, I HAVE TO RUN ON A TWO LANE highway that doesn't have a shoulder in order to access roads that are more suitable for running. Stares from drivers are plenty. Others shake their heads. Most courteously allow for a couple extra feet between me and their vehicle as they pass.

One afternoon, an elderly lady driving a 20 year old car that probably had less miles on it than my shoes, came to a stop as I approached. Her "only driven to church on Sunday" vehicle was in mint condition inside and out. As I drew closer on foot, she leaned over and manually cranked down the window on the passenger side. Assuming she was seeking directions, I stopped and bent down to the passenger side window. She promptly said, "One of these days you're gonna get run over out here!" I looked her in the eye and said, "Ma'am, as long as you know how to drive and I know how to run, everything should be just fine."

My intention was not to utter words that were dripping in sarcasm. But I could definitely see that they could be received that way. Her nose flew into the air as she squared up to the windshield, punched the accelerator, and proceeded down the highway at a rate of speed that car hadn't seen in some time.

Choose your words wisely. Be equally as wise in the way they're presented.

Psalm 19:14 reads, "Let the words of my mouth and the meditation of my heart be acceptable in Your sight, O Lord, my strength and my Redeemer."

Ephesians 4:29 is also a good reminder. "Let no corrupt word proceed out of your mouth, but what is good for necessary edification, that it may impart grace to the hearers."

12

Runner's Identity

Do it for long enough and people begin to identify you for what you are – a runner. It's not just friends and family. If people regularly see you pounding the pavement in your town, you can quickly establish that identity. And that's a good thing. Before you know it, everybody knows you're a runner. Okay, maybe not everybody.

A number of years ago, my training consistently took me through a certain neighborhood near our home. Some people saw me more often than their neighbors. I would typically cruise through the area twice in the afternoon, once at the start of my run, and then on my return home. One summer day, the afternoon forecast called for extreme heat and humidity, so I opted for an early morning run around 5 a.m. As I passed through, I noticed that a detached garage at one of the homes was on fire. I ran to the front door and pounded and pounded until the owner answered the door. I said, "Sorry to wake you, but your garage is on fire!" Still half asleep, he stepped out onto the porch, peeked around the corner of his house, then looked back at me, and said, "Oh my goodness, my garage is on fire!" Didn't I just tell him that? He wasted no time in calling the fire department. He also grabbed his car keys and made a beeline to the garage so he could pull his car out before it also fell victim to the flames.

When he came back, out of breath, waiting for the fire department to arrive, he said, "Could you please start putting my newspaper closer to the front porch so I don't have to walk all the way to the curb?" Yeah, he thought I was his paperboy.

Establish a running lifestyle and you will bear that runner's identity. And like those in Acts 11, I hope you've also established an upstanding Christian identity. The believers there worshipped Christ, the Messiah, and as it tells us in verse 26, "So it was that for a whole year they assembled with the church and taught a great many people. And the disciples were first called Christians in Antioch."

Let's see if you can also identify with these words from Jesus in John 13:34-35. "A new commandment I give to you, that you love one another; as I have loved you, that you also love one another. By this all will know that you are My disciples, if you have love for one another."

13

Faithfulness and Reward

BEING A CHILD OF THE 60'S AND GROWING UP IN THE STATE OF KANSAS, it was hard not to know about Jim Ryun. The sleek runner from Wichita became the first high school runner to break four minutes in the mile.

A few years later, Frank Shorter took the running world by storm, capturing the gold medal in the marathon at the 1972 Summer Olympics in Munich, Germany. Many credit Shorter for igniting the running boom in America in the 1970's.

Later that decade, Bill Rodgers became the poster boy for American running. Dubbed "Boston Billy," Rodgers won the Boston Marathon and New York City Marathon four times each from 1975 to 1980.

While each carried the torch for American distance running, they also had their own distinct running style. Ryun used a graceful stride with arms pumping and head bobbing as he distanced himself from would be challengers on the track. Shorter, his back upright, utilized classic form with very little wasted motion. And Rodgers, while graceful, had more bounce in his stride, his right arm sometimes looking more like he was conducting a symphony orchestra. However, they were very similar in that they believed in their abilities and had complete faith in their training. More often than not, victory was their reward.

In the same way, we find that God rewards faithfulness. In 2 John 8 it says, "Look to yourselves, that we do not lose those things we worked for, but that we may receive a full reward." Every believer has the potential of a full reward. The determining factor is our faithfulness to Christ.

Additional Suggested Scripture
Matthew 16:24-28

14

A Single Step

AS THE EXPRESSION GOES, "EVERY JOURNEY BEGINS WITH A SINGLE STEP."

So it was for Marty, a 37-year old schoolteacher. A disagreement with his wife sent Marty storming out the front door, his steps quick and forceful, the intensity in each stride the direct result of the confrontation he had just been part of. That night, his half mile trek around the neighborhood gave him a chance to cool off and clear his mind. He walked the next night as well...and the next...and the next. Fourteen months later, on the eve of his first 5K, Marty can't remember what the argument was about, but he knows it launched a fitness routine that changed his life.

So it was for Brock, an accomplished college athlete, who at 32 years old discovered that the "Battle of the Bulge" was more than just a German military offensive in World War II. Since graduation he concentrated more on climbing the corporate ladder than ascending the local high school's football stadium stairs. It was a company initiative to have healthier employees that led Brock to first step onto a treadmill at a local fitness center. Two years later, and more than 50 pounds lighter, he's stepping up to the starting line to compete in a grueling half marathon.

Each of us has our own story, some seemingly more compelling than others. It's a testimony that chronicles our running journey, and each began with a single step. So did our walk with Christ. Just as you recognized your need for physical change, you also recognized a spiritual void. John the Baptist and Peter gave us the starting point declaring with one simple word, "Repent." So did Jesus, who said in Mark 1:15, "Repent, and believe in the Gospel." And He says in Luke 13:3, "But unless you repent you will all likewise perish."

Praise God that we've taken that first step and that we continue on that blessed journey. If you haven't, I pray that you will today.

15

Running on Empty

As he entered the kitchen through the garage, Ben slammed the door behind him, making no effort to mask the disappointment he'd just experienced after running in a local 5K earlier that morning. He tossed a bag of fast food burgers and fries on the counter then reached inside the refrigerator to grab a nearly empty bottle of ketchup off the door. The container was turned upside down so what remained in the bottle was at the top.

Ben squirted some on a plate before the bottle made an unpleasant sound that led his wife to jokingly comment from an adjacent room, "I sure hope that was the ketchup bottle." It was, but he was in no mood for levity. Ben closed the container then forcefully pounded it into the palm of his hand, trying to get more ketchup into the top of the bottle. Again he squirted it onto his plate, soon followed by that sound, this time without his wife's commentary.

Later that evening, Ben realized his 5K performance was very similar to the ketchup bottle. He'd neglected his training over the last six weeks, and when he tried to make a move late in the race, there wasn't much left in the tank. He summoned a bit of a kick with about 400 meters to go, but it was short lived. Ben crossed the finish line, like an also-ran in the Kentucky Derby that faded badly during the stretch run.

Our faith can be like the contents of that ketchup bottle. It starts completely full, but over time the amount dissipates. We neglect our Bible reading and our prayer time, and before you know it, a crisis in our life has us turned upside down, as we try to muster every last ounce of faith left.

The running and racing equation requires faith in your training in order to achieve success. More important, trusting in the truth of God's Word brings reliability and stability to your Christian walk. Isaiah 40:8 reminds us, "The grass withers, the flower fades, but the Word of God stands forever."

Additional Suggested Scripture
Isaiah 41:10

16

Stop Running!

THE ROOM HAD REACHED ITS CAPACITY. EACH CHAIR WAS OCCUPIED, about 400 in all, with others standing around the perimeter ready to hear the evening's keynote speaker. Carter was one of those, having paid the additional $20 for the opportunity to enjoy the pre-race pasta meal and an inspirational message from a noted orator that travelled around the country to address runners the evening before their race.

Tonight's address would be different. The speaker, a devout Christian, having been invited to speak by the church sponsoring the 5K, began by saying, "Stop running! That's what I'm encouraging you to do tonight, stop running!" As he paused, throughout the room people looked at each other, wondering what direction this message was going to take.

Carter thought, "Is this guy kidding? Running has changed my life. I've never felt better. Number one, look at me. I've lost 45 pounds. My heart is stronger.

My cholesterol is lower. My blood pressure is back to normal. I fit in clothes I haven't been able to wear for years. Granted, they're out of style, but who cares, they fit! I've gone from a walk/run program to preparing for a marathon that's a couple of months away. And now you say stop running!"

The speaker continued, "Stop running from God!" Even the church's pastor was surprised by the topic, but now relieved with that clarification. "And no one in this room is exempt, even those who attend this church. Some of us in here are running from God simply because we have a love for sin. Others have established a bitterness towards God. It may be because of a tragic event in your life, a bad experience, or the loss of a loved one. Too many people judge God based solely on present circumstances, or something that's happened in their past. The truth is, in the process, you're running from a loving God who cares about you.

It says in 1 Peter 5:6-7, "Therefore humble yourselves under the mighty hand of God, that He may exalt you in due time, casting all your care upon Him, for He cares for you." The speaker noted that when you carry your worry and stress by yourself, it just shows that you haven't trusted God fully with your life. Carter knew exactly what he was talking about, having directed blame towards God when he lost his job late last year. Even now, in a job that pays a great deal less, the resentment was still there.

What are you running from? Is it sin in your life that continues to create separation between you and a loving God? Are you troubled by a dependence on alcohol or drugs that you're hiding from others? Are you in a relationship that you shouldn't be in? He loves you. He cares for you. Release that burden by giving it to Him, and stop running **from** God and begin running **to** Him. Remember what it says in Psalm 107:1, "Oh, give thanks to the Lord, for He is good! For His mercy endures forever."

17

Real Runners

THREE AND A HALF WEEKS AWAY FROM THE *DOZIER DASH* AND BILL Phalen found himself running 400 meter intervals on the local high school track. The "Dozier" was the city's featured 5K on the year's running calendar, attracting the best talent from a four state region. Bill was fine tuning, hoping to not only run a P-R on the relatively flat and fast "Dozier" course, but also to avenge a loss to a local rival who outkicked him down the stretch last year to claim the 40-44 age group title.

As he circled the track on his second 400, Bill was forced to lane three on the backstretch as he avoided two 30-something women walking leisurely on the inside lanes. Bill thought, "Aren't they aware of track etiquette? Don't they know to yield to *real* runners?" On his third and fourth 400s, he again went wide, avoiding the urge to verbalize his frustration. Twice more he retreated to lane three as he completed his fifth and sixth 400s before the ladies completed their "workout" and headed toward the parking lot.

Race day arrived and Bill reaped the reward of his intense training. He not only claimed victory in his age group, but surpassed his personal best 5K by more than eight seconds. Almost a half hour later, he watched as runners and walkers of all skill and fitness levels finished the course. That included the two ladies from the track. Bill applauded and shouted encouragement as they power-walked the course's final 50 meters. As the two crossed the finish line, hands raised triumphantly, Bill shared in their joy with more applause and an ear-piercing whistle. It was then that he recalled the sense of victory he felt, using a combination of running and walking, to complete his first 5K in just under 36 minutes.

It also brought to mind some Scripture his pastor shared in his sermon the previous Sunday. It was from Romans 12:3, "For I say, through the grace given to me, to everyone who is among you, not to think of himself more highly than he ought to think, but to think soberly, as God has dealt to each one a measure of faith."

Later that morning at the awards ceremony, his age group medal dangling from his neck, Bill heard the emcee announce that the race had raised over $15,000 for a local charity. He went on to thank the race's organizers, corporate sponsors, volunteers, and runners and walkers, recognizing that they all played a part in the success of the day's event. That led Bill back to Romans chapter 12 where it says in verses four and five, "For as we have many members in one body, but all the members do not have the same function, so we, being many, are one body in Christ, and individually members of one another."

18

Footsteps

LET'S FACE IT – YOU AND I TYPICALLY WITNESS THE WORLD'S BIGGEST sporting events in living color while sprawled out on our living room couch or relaxing in a recliner. Sure, we've dreamed of scoring that Super Bowl touchdown or hitting that World Series homerun, but we'll never find ourselves on one of those stages.

It was at the 2003 Chicago Marathon that I realized the uniqueness of road racing. My "preferred" starting position put me just 30 yards behind the "elite" runners, a contingent of Kenyans and a lone Moroccan, any of which could break the world record that very day. A world record – faster than any human had ever run that distance. The most prestigious marathoners on the planet toed the starting line, and I had the privilege of being a participant in this world class event, along with more than 40,000 other "also-rans." We shared the same course on that spectacular Chicago morning as my feet pounded the exact pavement over 26 miles as we ran past Wrigley Field, the Sears Tower, Soldier Field and along Lake Michigan before I dragged my weary body across the finish line more than an hour and a half later than that day's winner.

Thousands went before me that day. Thousands more followed behind me, all running the same course, with the finish line in beautiful Grant Park our ultimate destination. There, we congratulated each other, all proudly displaying the medals placed around our necks at the race's completion. Amazingly, each had their own unique perspective of the race as we passed through Chicago neighborhoods, and past its famed structures and landmarks.

As you read your Bible you find names like Moses, David, Job, Isaac, John and Paul. More recently we think of Christian notables like Chuck Swindoll and Billy Graham. Our walk with Christ has not brought us the notoriety they've experienced, but our goals are the same; to share the Gospel with those along our journey. And who will follow in your footsteps? In Psalm 79:13 it says, "So we, Your people and sheep of Your pasture, will give You thanks forever; we will show forth Your praise to all generations."

Additional Suggested Scripture
Hebrews 11:1-40

19

Comfort Zone

REMEMBER THAT PEACEFUL TRAINING RUN YOU DID ABOUT A WEEK AGO? It began in the cool, crisp morning air, with minimal traffic, and the next door neighbor in a robe and curlers, venturing out to retrieve the morning newspaper, thinking no one else was up yet.

Now it's race day, and that tranquility is nowhere to be found. It's been replaced by blaring music, colorful signage, and enough porta potties to accommodate the last minute relief efforts of hundreds, or even thousands of runners. It's exciting!

Your support staff is in place: your spouse and kids, your parents, even the in-laws, huddled together near the start to see you run the first 200 meters. If you're lucky, they'll catch a glimpse of you at one other spot along the course and at the finish armed with a homemade sign and a hearty yell of support.

Mile after mile, the crowds thin out and so do the runners. As you approach the 13 mile mark you realize you haven't heard a human voice since you passed through the last aid station, just the rhythmic pounding of your feet on the pavement. It's lonely and monotonous.

See any similarities with your Christian walk? Sunday mornings carry an excitement that parallels race day. Uplifting music, a beautifully decorated church, and familiar faces all put you in your Christian comfort zone.

But what about later in the week when you've distanced yourself from the church and congregation? At work or school, in a social setting, or even in your home, you face difficult decisions every day. Half way through that marathon you rely on the countless hours of training you put in preparing for race day. Don't settle for compromise in your daily life either. Rely on the Word of God and the spiritual training that will help you stay the course no matter what circumstances you may encounter.

Additional Suggested Scripture
John 5:24-25

20

Feel the Heat

The blistering summer sun has driven the afternoon temperature to nearly 100 degrees. High humidity simply multiplies the misery. The combination of the two creates an instant sweat the moment you depart the coolness of your home. Ten minutes into your daily run your head begins to pound, your body is zapped of its energy, and the scorching pavement even penetrates the soles of your shoes.

Common sense and a badgering wife were in agreement; take the day off. "Why do you need to run **every** day? It's not gonna kill you to take one day off!" But doesn't she and that little voice in my head know that I haven't missed a day of running in almost two years? So the temperature outside is more suited for a relaxing time in a sauna than for an eight mile run. "If you keel over and die, don't come running to me!" Out the door I go, from one heat to another. My "running travel-agent-of-a-wife" had reduced a leisurely eight mile run to a four mile guilt trip.

Is there a lesson here in common sense, or perhaps it's a matter of pride. In Proverbs 13:10 it says, "By pride comes nothing but strife, but with the well-advised is wisdom."

Like running, too often we turn things that are part of our Christian life, like Bible reading, prayer, and church attendance into an obligation rather than realizing that our relationship with Christ is a privilege that we should cherish. There is nothing more important in your life than your relationship with our Lord and Savior.

As for running, swallow some pride, wash it down with a drink from an ice cold bottle of your favorite sports drink, and don't be afraid to take a day off.

Additional Suggested Scripture

James 4:7-10

21

Game Day

WHAT A PICTURE PERFECT DAY. CONDITIONS ARE IDEAL. THE TEMPERATURE is a refreshing 51 degrees. 750 people anticipate the blast of the starter's pistol at 7 a.m.; the race photographer ready to capture them collectively as they stream toward the rising sun.

Now, it's ten minutes before race time. The announcer has instructed runners to assemble at the starting line, and as they do, anxiety sets in. A smorgasbord of emotions has just replaced the peacefulness I enjoyed as I warmed up. Have I trained enough? What if I go out too fast? Do I really want to do this? What if that guy in the cutoff jeans beats me? Why did I pay $25 to run 3.1 miles when I could have run it at home for free? Besides that, the race t-shirt is ugly. I'll never wear it!

There's no need to address all those questions, just the first one. Of course you've trained enough! You've logged the miles. You've done the speed work. Now, it's time to put yourself to the test. It's RACE DAY!

For runners, it's easy to identify RACE DAY. You've circled it on your calendar and then trained accordingly. The six, seven, or eight mile training runs and extra hill work were all in preparation for THAT DAY.

For Christians, GAME DAY is not that easy to pinpoint. Your Sunday morning church service IS NOT GAME DAY! Nor is your Wednesday night "care group." GAME DAY is sharing the Good News with a neighbor who's asking questions about your faith. GAME DAY is praying with a co-worker who just found out their spouse has cancer. It's counseling your children when they've made a poor decision, or comforting a friend who just lost their job.

Potentially, every day can be GAME DAY. And when those days come, remember the numerous times that Jesus exhibited "compassion" in Matthew, Mark, Luke and John. Psalm 145:8-9 says, "The Lord is gracious and full of compassion, slow to anger and great in mercy. The Lord is good to all, and His tender mercies are over all His works."

Be ready for GAME DAY and remember the example set by Jesus as you seize the opportunity to exhibit compassion.

Additional Suggested Scripture
2 Corinthians 1:3-4

22

Devil's Playground

OUR PASTOR REMINDED US ONE SUNDAY MORNING THAT "IDLE HANDS ARE the devil's playground." While that expression basically means that those who have nothing to do have a tendency to create mischief, it also reminds me why I typically run on busy thoroughfares when I train. Put me on a quiet country road or isolated trail and I'm more likely to be influenced by that small voice inside my head. You know the one. That not-so-big voice that tends to speak volumes. That's the one that continually tells me that "walking" is my friend, yet I know there's no benefit to giving in to that constant temptation. Why am I tempted? Because nobody's looking.

Pound the pavement amidst the traffic on a busy street and the temptation is greatly diminished. Why? Who wants to look defeated in full view of passing motorists? And answer this question, why is it that I occasionally have a few people say, "Hey, I saw you running the other day." But give in to that small voice just once and suddenly, every other person you encounter says "Hey, I saw you walking the other day."

Sometimes in our everyday existence we find ourselves detouring onto that quiet country road; that isolated trail, when that small voice tugs at our flesh. We're out of view of our family and friends, away from those in our congregation. Our pastor is none the wiser. Your secret's good. No concern about tarnishing your unblemished reputation.

Yet we know that you can't hide your actions from God. He's fully aware of your words and even your thoughts. Proverbs 5:21 says, "For the ways of man are before the eyes of the Lord, and He ponders all his paths."

The book of Ephesians helps us quickly realize that *our walk* is far more important than any run. In Ephesians 5:8-9 it says, "For you were once darkness, but now you are light in the Lord. Walk as children of light (for the fruit of the Spirit is in all goodness, righteousness, and truth), finding out what is acceptable to the Lord."

Additional Suggested Scripture
1 Corinthians 10:13

23

The Taste of Victory

PLATTSBURG IS A QUIET TOWN IN NORTHWEST MISSOURI WITH A population of just over 2300. Its greatest distinction however, is not who lives there, but who's buried there. Believe it or not, you can visit the gravesite of a former President of the United States. It's not Washington, Jefferson or Lincoln. Nor is it Roosevelt, Jackson or even Rutherford B. Hayes. At this point you must be thinking it's Missourian Harry S. Truman, but that would be incorrect as well. The correct answer is David Rice Atchison. The year was 1849, and history shows that Mr. Atchison was indeed "President for a day."

On this particular Saturday morning in Plattsburg, conditions were ideal for the 5K run/walk. The starting line was at the local high school before the course took us through this quaint town in the Show Me State that boasts some beautiful Victorian homes. As I sized up the competition gathered near the starting line, I thought

I might have a chance to finish in the top five. When you're in your mid 40's, that's a victory in itself.

The gun sounded and about 75 runners and walkers began a human stampede that may have had the former president rolling over in his grave. Less than a half mile into the race, it was apparent that this was a rather weak field. I assumed the lead, with another guy matching me stride for stride at about a six minute a mile pace. As we made our way toward the mile marker, a Plattsburg resident opened his front door, and out ran the most vicious Rottweiler I'd ever seen, making a beeline for the front runners in this race, one of which happened to be me. Thank God the owner's yell made this ferocious looking Fido retreat just as he got within a few feet of us.

Over the next half mile, I put some distance between me and the other gentleman, following the pace car which guided me through a number of residential neighborhoods. I settled into a comfortable pace, looking back as I turned each corner to see if anyone was closing the gap that I'd worked so hard to create. Surprisingly, no one was. But there was a surprise ahead of me.

Ready to taste victory, despite a mouthful of fumes from the pace car, I made the final turn toward home only to see, about a quarter mile in the distance, my running companion back at the mile mark, breaking the tape at the finish line to the thunderous applause of a small crowd that had gathered.

What happened? Did the guy in the pace car take me for a ride? Gone was my victory and the $50 cash prize that went with it. Discouraged, I slowed my pace as I completed the course, now not so pleased with my second place finish. The crowd's applause sounded more polite than thunderous as I crossed the finish line.

My questions were quickly answered just a few feet beyond the finish line as the apparent "victor" met me and informed me that he'd taken a wrong turn. The shortcut shaved about a half mile off the course, and although inadvertent, it led to his disqualification.

Many people believe that there are a number of roads that lead to heaven. Please know the truth. Jesus tells us in Matthew 7:13-14, "Enter by the narrow gate; for wide is the gate and broad is the way that leads to destruction, and there are many who go in by it. Because narrow is the gate and difficult is the way which leads to life, and there are few who find it."

Having entered by that narrow gate, I'm guaranteed victory through Christ Jesus. And although I haven't won any road races since, like David Rice Atchison, I'm glad to say that this dog has had his day.

Additional Suggested Scripture
Luke 15:11-32

24

Going Downhill

THE ENGLISH LANGUAGE IS DEFINITELY COMPLEX. MAYBE CONFUSING would be a better way to describe it. We've got words that we spell the same and pronounce the same, but they have different meanings. Then there are words that we pronounce the same but spell differently, and words we spell the same but then pronounce a different way. And then there are expressions that are just as baffling like "to look a gift horse in the mouth" and "kill two birds with one stone," which by the way, has nothing to do with any species of our feathered friends.

As a runner, consider the expression "going downhill." In American culture, that typically has a negative connotation. It would indicate that your circumstances have taken a turn for the worst: you lost your job, your physical condition is deteriorating, your mother-in-law is moving in with you. Things have gone from good to bad.

But for a runner "going downhill" is just the opposite. After ascending a difficult grade, we've reached the top, and now it's time for our reward. "Going downhill" allows us to relax, recover, and to run with less effort. Our circumstance has definitely improved. But it took faith on your part to arrive at the summit, knowing that your training would take you to the top of that hill for your reward.

In our Christian walk, we are encouraged in Colossians chapter three to "seek those things which are above, where Christ is, sitting at the right hand of God." Your perseverance and faith in your training brought you to your reward as you conquered that hill. Your faith in God will bring a much greater reward. Hebrews 11:6 reminds us, "But without faith it is impossible to please Him, for he who comes to God must believe that He is, and that He is a rewarder of those who diligently seek Him."

Additional Suggested Scripture
Matthew 21:21-22

25

Hands and Feet

Imagine the famous chef Emeril Lagasse never having prepared a meal for another person, but rather, confining his culinary abilities to his own kitchen. Or imagine that the world never knew the incredible acting abilities of Morgan Freeman, or the artistic talents of Norman Rockwell. Imagine that we never got to see Jack Nicklaus hit a golf ball or heard Billy Graham deliver a sermon. We all would have been denied something that God intended to bless us with.

He's also gifted you in a way that is intended to bless others. You may never have thousands packing into a stadium or millions watching you on television. Instead, God may have designed you to simply touch the lives of those in your home, in your neighborhood, your kids' school, or right now, it could be just one life. Your gift may be an ear that listens, or a shoulder to cry on, a compassionate embrace, a warm smile, or a bag of groceries. As it tells us in the book of Ephesians, "redeem the time," and capitalize on every appropriate opportunity.

1 Corinthians 12:4-6 reminds us, "There are diversities of gifts, but the same Spirit. There are differences of ministries, but the same Lord. And there are diversities of activities, but it is the same God who works all in all."

Isn't it amazing that God has created and gifted each of us uniquely. Jeremiah 29:11 reminds us that God has a plan for each of us. It says, "For I know the thoughts that I think toward you, says the Lord, thoughts of peace and not of evil, to give you a future and a hope."

And what an honor and a privilege it is to use those gifts for God's glory. In Philippians 2:12-13 it says, "Therefore, my beloved, as you have always obeyed, not as in my presence only, but now much more in my absence, work out your own salvation with fear and trembling; for it is God who works in you both to will and to do for His good pleasure."

Whatever your gifts are, whatever God's will is for your life, express your love for running by being God's hands and feet.

26

Boston or Bust

STEVE FURLER PACED ANXIOUSLY AMONG HIS FELLOW COMPETITORS NEAR the starting line. This wasn't his first marathon. In fact, four months earlier he'd completed his sixth. But today's 26 mile test had greater importance for Steve. Having turned 50 the month before, he knew a three hour and 30 minute marathon was now the qualifying standard for him to achieve his goal of competing in the prestigious Boston Marathon.

Steve was confident in his ability to conquer the distance. He'd done it six times before. As he bent at the waist to touch is toes, he saw the timing chip attached to his shoe, the small device that would contain the data that could help him mark Boston off his running bucket list.

Three miles into the race, Steve was right on schedule. His sub-eight minute miles produced the pace he needed to punch his ticket to Bean Town. At the six mile mark, Steve felt great, still maintaining his pace and utilizing each aid station to keep his body hydrated. Despite rising temperatures, Steve held his sub-eight pace and even extended his stride on a gradual downhill near the halfway point of the race.

Miles 17, 18 and 19, and Steve was on schedule, his only discomfort was the sting in his eyes from the sweat that ran from his forehead. With less than six miles to go, the number of runners overcome by the demands of the race were multiplying. Some chose to stop, others resorted to walking. One, about 50 meters in front of him, staggered in the street, seemingly disillusioned. His legs wobbled, and the closer Steve came to him, the less control he had over his body. Other runners passed by, trying to avoid his lethargic state. But Steve, 26 years a paramedic, recognized the danger that existed.

As he came alongside him, Steve looked at the man's face and suggested he take a break. Steve helped him to the curb and laid him down in the grass, his head now resting in Steve's lap. He was a man in his mid 40's, his body tanned from months of training, but now his face became a pale white. This far into the race, there were no spectators in the area, so Steve summoned an oncoming runner to request medical help at the next aid station which was less than 200 meters away. Steve shaded the man's head as much as he could and maintained conversation as the two awaited medical personnel. About 12 minutes later, Steve looked up the road and saw an ATV heading their way, and medical assistance was moments away.

As they arrived, Steve gave a quick update on the situation, received thanks from his new friend Josh, and pulled himself up from the ground. His once fresh legs were now stiff, and as he bent over to stretch his body, he noticed the timing chip on his shoe. He realized that his Boston dream for now would be put on hold.

Steve walked to the aid station, thanking God with every step for the opportunity to serve, knowing that there would be other marathons. Despite finishing in just over three hours and 50 minutes, his seventh marathon was his most satisfying. As he told his story to friends and family later than evening, he was inundated with modern day "good Samaritan" references. It also brought to mind some Scripture he'd read earlier in the week in Philippians 2:3-4, "Let nothing be done through selfish ambition or conceit, but in lowliness of mind let each esteem others better than himself. Let each of you look out not only for his own interests, but also for the interests of others."

26.2

I Am a Runner/I Am a Christian

I am a runner. I have the body of an athlete.
I am a Christian. I have the mind of Christ. (1 Corinthians 2:16)

I am a runner. I stay fit to prolong life.
I am a Christian. "And this is the promise that He has promised us – eternal life." (1 John 2:25)

I am a runner. My intense training helps me to endure.
I am a Christian. "For the joy that was set before Him, He endured the cross." (Hebrews 12:2)

I am a runner. My passion for running requires great commitment.
I am a Christian. I desire to love the Lord my God with all my heart, with all my soul, with all my strength, and with all my mind. (Mark 12:30)

I am a runner. I train diligently for one reason – to get faster. I thrive on speed.

I am a Christian. "Let every man be swift to hear, slow to speak, slow to wrath; for the wrath of man does not produce the righteousness of God." (James 1:19-20)

I am a runner. I trust my training to help me complete any course.

I am a Christian. "Trust in the Lord with all your heart, and lean not on your own understanding. In all your ways acknowledge Him, and He shall direct your paths." (Proverbs 3:5-6)

I am a runner. Although I train diligently, I may never win a race.

I am a Christian. "But thanks be to God, who gives us the victory through our Lord Jesus Christ." (1 Corinthians 15:57)